A STICK THAT BREAKS AND BREAKS

A STICK THAT BREAKS AND BREAKS

MARIANNE BORUCH

Oberlin College Press

Publication of this book was made possible in part by a grant from the Ohio Arts Council.

Library of Congress Cataloging-in-Publication Data

Boruch, Marianne, 1950-
      A Stick That Breaks and Breaks / Marianne Boruch.
      (The FIELD Poetry Series v. 5)
      I. Title.   II. Series.

LC: 97-066614
ISBN: 0-932440-79-7
      0-932440-80-0 (pbk.)

Contents

For my mother, and for Michael

OMENS

First thought, the roof's edge and a bird there, singing.
Second, slight fissure in the egg.
Then I noticed light: tornado light, my husband said.
Yellowish. Unblinking. Fourth and fifth, how either shoe
would work, left for right, and so on.
Sixth, a boy sitting at the curb, just sitting. I forget
what seventh was. Then the egg
opened so I could see it. Ninth—the beak, no, the tip
of the beak, past shell. Tenth was everything
lost to sacrifice: the grungy cat fallen, rabbits freezing
in the yard that winter; and crushed by cars, frogs
day by day down to their gritty nothing, or nothing's
pure abstraction. Eleven was
the sound of that: three bells, but mostly after.
You could hear it like you breathe at night
but the thing moving was a moth, in cupboards and closets, wings
done in pen and ink, and done again. And done again.
And done again.

•••

So I kept seeing oddball things—old catholic in me
falling down a well. Rethink another omen: small wound
I never noticed but the scar is there
a lifetime. I remember working in a bank,
so bored the summer I was twenty I'd imagine customers
shrunk back to whatever child they came from, easy,
in diapers, or some had holsters, shirts
that snapped, racing up and down—such joy—

in circles. They'd loom at my window then, grown up,
all business. I'd count out what they wanted, knowing
one thing true about them, fished from the crevice only
boredom loves and loves. That egg opens
because a thing wants out. A thing with feet and feathers.
Swollen shut, eyes that make
the whole head wobble on a stalk. How *does*
one cell, dividing? Ancient rope
on rope. Blueprints dream the house, or—
marriage, man or woman, leaf or sparrow, seasick coral,
ragged goat, river rat that knows the rain-soaked alleys
inside out, beloved goldfinch, dear destructive
neighbor boy, puffer fish....

•••

I'll give you omen #17—as far as I can go with it. After years,
a visit back, a childhood friend, her mother's kitchen, washer,
dryer to the left as we sat below a skylight never opened,
dusky, murky day from that. Her mother nodded
toward the virgin's statue beaming bland contentment
from atop the dryer. And halfway through her terrible rendition,
her husband's death, said, *I was so lost*
without him, pointing, *then*
the blessed mother moved her hand. The man
helped me once, when my father threw my brother out, how
he drove me everywhere that night in snow—not a single
question—to find where my brother, barefoot, ran mile
on mile. So close to sobbing, talk's not
right, nothing's right. Compassion's
not a simple angel but in that darkened car, its shine
was quiet, how every low, familiar house and street
swept by. *Look*, she said, *my hand is*
shaking. Fierce guardian of the neighborhood, her eyes

on mine—agnostic—until
I nodded. Meanwhile, placid, frozen, *she* gazed toward us still
from high Mt. Dryer where below our tiny lives wound
and rewound, backward, forward. Molded shape, plastic
someone poured on an assembly line. A billion,
million Marys just like her. *I saw it, my own eyes.*
I saw it. So swore farmers, kings and hermits, clerks
and teachers, artists, merchants, anyone
sick to death or shattered.... I believed something
sitting there, believed such is sorrow's stone
and ache, that we imagine
every end to it. *I feel peace*, she said. *Like he's*
happy there, wherever. Blueprints in the genes, house
that rises secretly.

So often as a kid I'd lie in bed
and watch my hand turning toward the window.
And play *x-ray*, seeing bone, past
bone to throbbing marrow. Days turn like that
to light. Any omen
is x-ray. Its lens let down
a quiet through the gauzy skylight, quiet
from the car that found my brother one night in snow, shine
without clarity to flood that kitchen. So a dryer
was an altar. So what. So I took her hand across the table,
anyone would, all the sleepless
this for that, the welling up where
no words know.

•••

But the moment right before—I want back
to that: the cat careful but the long-shot branch complaining, slow
splintering one barely hears. Or the rabbit stretched

in briefest flight. Or frogs
on some ordinary mission, simply crossing roads
for water, summer's twilight, whatever frogs wisely, dumbly do.
Omen 20: the bus this morning lowers pitch as it rounds
the hill. Then someone's hammer quickens
in the valley, nail that doesn't
love the wood, not really, but still
the house goes up. Or this—a dream one night
that flashed me frozen
out of dream, exactly as a life goes out, forget
how many years. It was Odysseus who watched eagles pitch
and hover, marveled at the omen, who was told in a waking dream
to walk inland far enough from water to lose
his sorrow, far enough that anyone would mistake his oar
for a farmer's tool, a thing to winnow wheat.
That such wheat is the color
of my child's hair, or the light my husband waits for
in certain storms, means—
nothing much, though lying there, jarred
awake that way,
I told myself things.

I

MOMENTARY, IN WINTER

It is colder. More people
in the muffin shop, more now in the library
including the oldest man
I have ever seen. How he sits
so happily and turns the page. What is it
he reads? I can't make it out.

But some good someone has built a fire here.
Call it *hearth*, a word part heart,
part breath, a first last
gasp, the final surprise where a mouse
jumps out of a mouse and shocks
the poor cat.

Poor warm cat. Because we stare
into the fire, and then the page.
But this book on my lap is
a liar—book about flowers, it's all
about failure. Momentary fold, foolish
blinding color in the day's
half gloom. Winter is
too many books upon the table—
thick books and skinny books, a book
of destinations: Spain, amazing
untouched villages in Spain....

From the street, I saw two women
in the muffin shop. Steam

rose from their cups and changed
their faces so subtly I thought how
pleasure is nothing and then
unlocks: not like a clock does, not
how wings or ribbons do.

Oh, blame the cold. There was
a window.

LENT

The second week of Lent I walked
under crows fine in their
calamity, the wide dark wings, the heavy
rusted hinge in their throats.
I heard them once,
twice, too many times. They were a cloud
of bad hooks coming down, complaining.
The path lay ahead and went up,
mostly mud, but water
moved quick under ice, the sound
of anyone crying, then door after door
closing against it. So the light
gauzed over early, from 4 o'clock on.
Lent because of that, or because
of the branches, still spiny and bare.
Into the old leaves of summer I read
oak and *black willow* pressed
into the furrows, the half-frozen bootprints.
Lent because I kept walking, or because
I hadn't slept.

Always, one is told things
after a death: *the woods*
will give way to a field, or *grief*
has its own sweetness, or
she will come to you in a dream
if you ask. But it was all thicket
where I walked, one woodpecker

circling and circling the same
dead tree, probing and listening.
He never left the high wood.
Finally is a word like stone, like
water. Or opening like water and closing
like stone. And finally the woods
opened to a field. I saw
a family there
before distance swallowed them.
I saw their bright coats
get smaller, the children
lagging behind, the mother
turning back to them and speaking.

It's Lent, I told myself, as if
this were reason. For a long time
I watched for larks in the half-light
where tall grass
was bent and tousled like the hair
of a child after sleep.
Love is a wheel and a weight. Once
I slept perfectly, not knowing.

HALFWAY

I hear cars. I hear crows. I hear
the house taking the cold and making it
a bone breaking. All winter these stairs,
and we both give way—my leg
which sings out at knee or hip,

and the wood remembering someone cut
and dragged it to a darker place,
split it into brothers and took from it
its sisters. It could have been a coffin.
Or kept for cheap crates, being pine.

Tomatoes would have given
their summer blood to it. But it was led.
It was laid down straight
to stop all falls. Oddest of places,
neither up nor down. I whisper

to the stairs. Gratitude
is never loud. I praise the awful days
of its becoming. I praise the sapling
buried here. Back of that, the seed
which sent up heartbreak. It broke in half

on purpose. And before, before
the tiny cone wept its resin, the pine
took light from shade to climb
and climb. I wasn't there, but back of praise
is sorrow. Halfway, halfway up the stairs.

In The Street, Men Working

Flares make an altar here,
roaring water from the broken main, rushing
weird procession, sacrifice to all thirst,
to those who'd trade anything
for rain.
        Cars move by, awkward,
missing the sputtering light
by inches. The men glare back, but the hole
opened in the street, they
look down the way
surgeons consider the heart
draped on all sides by sheets, the extraordinary
pulsing heart.
        Early morning.
People taking out trash come over. Kids
bored vacant on their way to school stop
and merely want the great ho-hum
of everything to lift. The street's
whole secret self
is rising—so what if it's busted.
Son-of-a-bitch, the men
say to each other softly, for
nerve, a thing
mindless and heroic
as love.
        The soul descends
reluctantly such depths. The others, watching

from the rim—not sympathy exactly
but a dread so pure and mute
it slips past them, into air,
a scent.

SEWING

My mother was sewing: pajamas for us, always,
and curtains for the window
to sleep in. At night she pulled them loose
against the wide backyard where the dog
roamed from plum tree to willow, where
the hammock hung in shade.

But all of it was shade at night
except the moon's full face.
Small umbrellas on my flannel, small
pirates on my brother's as if in dreams
it rained too much
and enough ships docked there
for a whole childhood's worth of thieves.

Years, the same room, the same window.
My brother's bed there and my bed there.
And arguments between us like a wheel
turned to make the other go,
as though one engine.

In the dark, I heard her sewing. Each stitch
a splinter put back and back so rapidly.
Not song exactly. Not pain.
It's the little wizard wayward spool I still
think about, high
and quick—the way it almost
flew, but turned to make and make.

Camouflage

The butterfly is the eye
of some greater creature, if we
believe the wing,
the brilliant circle which
watches and watches, waits for
its grisly chance. It's
                    all disguise.
Or the way even sparrows
fluff and rear up
to be bigger. Bigger than
any other tiny bird,
bigger than the next day,
or the day after that
with its freezing rain,
departing berry.
                    So the mimics come—
the starling, the mocking bird
which over and over can be anything at all:
a crow or a dove, a riff
of Mozart—scary beast—or a car door
slamming.
            Deception *because*. Deception
since the Ice Age for some.
Secrets in the bones which aren't
whispers, in the fine
and serious brain
whose best parts
cannot think.

                    Birds that hiss
from the nest like snakes
so the heart fails
even in a hawk.
                            And our own
big cars. Dangerous night, eyes
that blind a deer, stop it
senseless. Not an angel
wielding fire....

CHINESE BRUSHWORK

It's their silence that pools. Then afterwards
students blackening the basins with their inks,
washing off all that concentration. It's
a matter of walking by, nothing in my hands
and finding them deliberately
touching the paper the ancient way, these kids
with their caps on backwards, hair
tied with a band. In the women's john, they hardly
speak above the water rushing the black stones,
the sable brushes. Every Tuesday and Thursday,
their teacher peering over each hunched shoulder
as they do leaves, or they do rivers, or they do
the apple beginning to decay. Ink has its
own creature life, one drop a sudden
artery. The heart isn't far. I held my brush like this,
foolish and solemn, bent like this,
slightly panicked, the old man who taught
bent in turn over us, holding his cigarette high,
taking in smoke, letting it out, curious bellows.
His hardly any English, simply pointing—*too thin* or
not dark enough—our lines leading
waywardly up to make a place to see from. I think
of those puzzles a child might do
slow, in a fever, the world bit by bit—someone
fishing, say, below mountains and trees,
the vast silver of the lake unfurling, an expanse
utterly without detail, dawn or just after
and the teacher's hand on my hand—*no, this,*

this—as he shook his head briefly
like a bird, like someone giving up. I liked
making pears best because some shapes
are comic, some resist you and look back.
I remember my inkstone, rinsing
as these young women do, the long line of sinks
and standing there above the wide black circling
toward the underworld and reaching for the paper towel
and thinking nothing but how I'd felt
the hour pass as a rock feels light, I mean
not feeling it at all. Every time now
I want to speak to them about this fine
and worthless thing they do, Tuesdays and Thursdays,
maybe even at home in the kitchen or at a dormitory desk,
rivers that go on and vines that take the paper
as though it were a place for thought and thought
could climb. Deep contrast—as if that dream
were ever true, the fruit offered again and again
to the frozen instant. It isn't death I feel, walking
by their classroom or seeing the young women
at the sinks, seeing them and seeing how the mirror
gives them back. Something else, though I haven't
a name for it—this thing that opens dumbly
into another thing. A moment, or a shape
that endlessly repeats itself, the way,
walking alone, one who never expects to be loved
might say a name to the open air, and each time
it is hopeless, it is lovely, it is secret.

CRUSHED BIRDS

So many crushed birds in the street.
I don't know why it rains so
taking the small bodies
down to their bones, just a few
but they are silver.

Day by day, more fall—
a sparrow, a young cardinal
not yet
his true color. Sometimes the head
is perfect, the eye
glossy, no failure in its depths.
It's the wings
that are shattered, as if
in flight, gravity gave way, the sky itself
throwing down this thing
passing through it.

There was one I couldn't
recognize: bits of muscle
tied to bone, a few
feathers awry. Even a cat
would complain. In rain, it looked
washed by every human sadness,
not a heart or a thought, more
what aches and aches—those times
I stood there
and could not speak, didn't say....

HAPPINESS

In the old tapestry, how they float
among the flowers, queen and servants both,
all equally. The vast blue
behind lily and rose
is their permanent element, not as sky
or water makes a world, but as
childhood does, wishing the day
would last. An honest-to-god queen
wouldn't like it, really, such weightlessness,
her servants aloft like birds,
obedient birds, just
barely. All this is
dream—ours, when we think about the past.
Or it might be the weavers'
simple ignorance of perspective.
As if ignorance were ever simple.
And happiness? I look
into the faces of the queen and all
her servants, or at how their bodies
take the scented air of centuries.
They're oblivious—to the flowers set skyward
and adrift, to anything but
looking blankly out. The weavers making such eyes
had to drop one thread and let
the endless backdrop blue
leak in. Perhaps it was a sweet thing, emptying
their heads like that. Now each is so light

all rise and rise.
They don't know where they are, what
land, or who
the enemy.

NESTING BOXES

Going into fall, I made
nesting boxes in our small dim basement
thinking what birds
come out of nowhere: one called
Mischief, and one called
Remorse. One called *Sadness-that-is-*
Lifting-Even-as-I-Pound-the-Nails.
I measured badly, cut.
And measured over. Still the boxes
came forth graciously
in spite of me. Then I was raising
a ladder to the maple, to the old garage
where eaves begin. I walked
right up to the arbor, the part
that isn't leaning.
                    What is it
in a box like that? Longing. Or something
worse, further back.
I nailed the last wall
and darkness filled it like air.
I put my eye to it—
a disturbance, bad
weather looming.
                    And spring? Of course
it was blinding. And the darkness
cried out to them, the wrens,
the chickadees. I watched

them disappear in it, their
slowed, blurred bodies
seconds before—

CAR COVERED WITH SNOW

Before I clear the windows, I sometimes
sit inside. And the stillness is such
that I lose how the day works.
It soaks up
all the steely details: March
ripped out of February, a raw thing.
Sometimes my son has patience.
And we sit a few minutes like this
in the weird half-light. He says: *we're*
in a closed fist, Mama.
Or, *it's like the car's eye is closed.*
We're deep in the brain then,
seeing as the blind see, all
listening. Outside, the cardinal
tinks tinks his alarm call,
his scared call. I hear it: the snow
so terribly white.
And he is brilliant,
conspicuous.

The Vietnam Birthday Lottery, 1970

Not winter still, but not
quite spring, and any hope narrowed
to the dorm's TV
in the lounge downstairs, the official
gravel of its voice. And girls
in scattered chairs, not languid or wise-ass for once,
not distracted. Such a little screen: black
and white, and men who moved only
their mouths, in suits that made them
bigger. But the girls kept track,
and each had a birthday
hidden in that quiet like a flame
you'd cup a hand around,
in wind. The wind
was history and its filthy sweep, whatever
rots like that, in one head
or a thousand. On this day, all days
turned a tragic swift ballet. And thinking as I did
no *what if*, no boyfriend, nothing
staked directly in the heart to stay
and stay, I thought merely
a kind of cloud
filled the room, or smoke. You could see it
and smell it: everyone dark-dreaming there alone
though—what?—twenty, thirty of us?
The only light
was dread, one small window of it, with its
vacant men on the other side

poised above the spinning box like those
cheap quiz shows, and you could get
a gleaming washer or a spiffy car, an Oldsmobile
with any luck. Of course
you could. Of course, sobbed my friend
whose boy was suddenly born all wrong,
right on target, though, that moment, illegal
as an angel, already half
stupefied by visions
on a fake i.d. in some bar downtown. The whole
night like that: sobbing
or relief, dead drunk either way.
I fell asleep late to the boys'
roaring home, broken
wayward lines of them, the marked
and the saved, by moonlight or streetlight.
I can't remember which.

THE BOOK OF HAND SHADOWS

An eagle and a squirrel. A bull and a sage.
All take two hands, even the sheep
whose mouth is a lever for nothing, neither
grass nor complaint. The black swan's
mostly one long arm, bent
at the elbow but there's always feathers
to fool with. Front leaf: a boy
with a candle, leaning curious while
an old man makes
a Shakespeare. The small pointed beard
is a giveaway.
                    I always wanted to, especially
because of the candle part. How the eye is finally
a finger bent to make an emptiness. Or that
a thing thrown up there
is worlds bigger than how it starts. So I liked
the ceiling better than the wall, looking up
where stars roamed and moon sometimes
hovered, were the roof lost,
were we lucky
and forgot ourselves.

I Notice On My Walk

the person sitting funny in a chair, drawing
by pencil or pen in the old summer grass—
late winter here, mostly
thawed. Male or female, I can't
tell. I see the small head
bending. I see the arm
like a tiny gear in some
slow watch that goes
and goes.
               Hardly much light—
clouds took it. Hardly any wind
in the meadow. A person drawing like that
is a glimpse or a shiver, a moment
falling out of itself to stop
the afternoon. Still, he
or she is drawing—
what? The high crooked grass,
the light on the grass, the mind
on the light on the grass.
                     I take the long
way around, as if this were
my orbit. The miraculous hand
is quick and quiet
at the center. Old moon, I tell myself,
because it's getting dark, or because
I love the distance.

SWIMMING LESSON

At his lesson, the child cannot
stop weeping. The huge instructor takes him in his arms
to sure disaster, across the ropes
and back, and across
while the other kids get smaller, sitting
on the edge, bored
or terrified, waiting out their chance: it's all
a watery blur to him.
My son and I on the other side
take turns at diving
for the rings—blue and red and yellow
in the water which magnifies
everything but sound. An hour or so, we
squint and glide, giants
to each other, slow motion
in the ancient underwater: *we*
bestride the world, and so on.
But even near the bottom, the ring
almost in my fingers, I hear it—the weeping
endlessly, like a stick that breaks
and breaks, like a starless night in summer
when all there is
is the roaring body's pulse—as the little boy
is carried from half this world
to the other half, his instructor doing
an awkward *it's okay* and *see how nice*
the water is until it's some
blonde girl's turn. Surely it is better

on the solid ledge. But still
he cries and cries. Poor child who knows
what he knows, and we are
fools. Pretty afternoon. Cloudless sky.

THE AUCTION

The barn roof turned our secret wide
and sloping as the distance a star might realize
through the tilting summer dark, though
it was day, the sleepless stretch
of afternoon. Below, the yard
laid out for auction: furniture
and boxes in the grass, bed linens, sheet music,
this life and the next. My great aunt walked
among it all, months past
any what or where. I swear she thought it
a garden, not iris or lily or rose,
but she traced the lines of wood
and china tenderly, as one
goes anonymous before
the sealed leaf. Someone
had forgotten her. Or someone
was busy. We were busy
on the roof, cousins so young
even girls were boys, throwing off
our shirts, fierce, careless because the oak
was massive shade. So small
down there, my aunt
wavering, her hand slowly to her ear, as if
I could call to her
from that roof, or from here.

THE GREAT APE HOUSE

In winter, the smell got worse. It took you like
a soup. The giant glass-eyed ape would stare with such
condescension I could feel again, walking in
out of freezing wind, how small even my largest
bones—poor femur in the thigh, shoulder blades—
though in that look I passed
quickly to ribs, delicate, barely thicker
than my breathing. I could hear
my heart. And closer to the glass, others
come to see him, taunting, screwing up
their human faces to be, they thought,
just like his. I was quiet. I was, so help me, empty
as the great savanna. But apes love trees.
Banana, more bananas. I watched him toss aside the peel
exactly like my British colleague, years later
in Taiwan, would drop her cigarette on our
office floor, saying, no dear, *they'll*
pick it up—when her tiny daughter
went for it. But not exactly that, since his
was an honest kingdom, fallen grace. The ape would
turn away, though not for long. Or he'd languidly climb
and do some nonchalant miracle, rope to rope.
But not for long. He'd come back, stand
and look at us. Rain or snow outside,
everything whirled and narrowed to just
that look. Like taking your eye to a telescope's eye
and losing it there, up the long dark
in hope of stars. The light, always bad, mounds

of hay, old cabbage heads, carrot leaf.
An attendant would call to him from the upper story.
But he'd keep that look for us, looking at some
distant shape inside himself the way one might think
a swollen river marks something in a dream.
Or so I thought, since thinking is mostly
trying not to drown. I know I spent
too long in there. But I was twenty.

THE HAWK

He was halfway through the grackle
when I got home. From the kitchen I saw
blood, the black feathers scattered
on snow. How the bird bent
to each skein of flesh, his muscles
tacking to the strain and tear.
The fierceness of it, the nonchalance.
Silence took the yard, so usually
restless with every call or quarrel—
titmouse, chickadee, drab
and gorgeous finch, and the sparrow haunted
by her small complete surrender
to a fear of anything. I didn't know
how to look at it. How to stand
or take a breath in the hawk's bite
and pull, his pleasure
so efficient, so *of course, of course*,
the throat triumphant,
rising up. Not
the violence, poor grackle. But the
sparrow, high above us, who
knew exactly.

SNOW FALLING

Before midnight it began and now
early morning, still
it is falling. The muffled crows. The loud cars
I can barely hear.
Inside the white apple
are the smallest seeds and I was told once
they were poison. Only the thickest
of the bare trees darken.

There's a thought like this which took
all night to settle: snow
that comes and comes, whether you
dream or not.

Everything in gauze. When a car passes
it is a puncture wound, a brief
tiny show of blood.
So much snow
one can't see where the street
rides rough-shod, where
the curb refuses.

STAINED GLASS WINDOWS

The colors so rich
one forgets how
terrible these visions.

Angels who come brilliantly out of the dark—
one there, buoyed up by cloud
still offering Christ the goblet
in the garden.
One supplies the word: *drink.*
No hand goes up for it. Not yet.
In the pause, I go past thinking.

But old men always hold infants
and make prophecies. They hear the world
ticking. Dread is seeded
across the pews, on the other side.
And such surprise in the faces
as the elder speaks
and touching the pale child, reads
the years ahead like rain
he can see through.

In the garden, only the sky
really tells: crooked and exact
every piece, deep red going
black. How a wound stains.
How we love
to look at it.

BIRD PASSING

My ears hurt. And I read a book
about the passenger pigeon, thousands in a single tree
and the tiny man in the engraving, outstretched
as a beggar or a saint looking up—
except his rifle and his leer and his 50 lb. net.
The turn of the century: a massive
groan, years on years rolling over like some
sleepy drunk. The dream of the past
is addictive. My grandparents
down there in their 20s, late teens, thrilled
as anyone to write *three*
new digits.... I'm sick

about the passenger pigeon. Once, in the Field Museum
I stopped before a few last
real ones stuffed high and low in their
phony, life-sized tree
behind the glass. Late eighteen hundred
and something. Not long. Maybe
20 years in the countdown, the museum bag slipping
over their heads, not
some kid fooling around
with a blanket. I tried to believe
in their sweetness, lovely anything
doomed. I can't lie. That red eye could
pierce an eye. It was glass, sure. But even
books make that stare famous, the sleaziest

trapper, the sort who'd crush each
head by hand under the net, hundreds—even he
would turn away. Clearly these
were stragglers. No longer monstrous clouds, thick strata
upon strata of them passing overhead—8 or 9
or 14 hours' blackened daylight, horses
trembling in harness, guns raised to quell
whatever astonishment. One shot, it's said 300
would fall, stunned as stone in planted fields
or open meadow. And mostly
left. That's the blistering fact—left there,
bone and feather and failing muscle, thousands
and thousands of others airborne,
for the moment. Eventually hundreds of others.
Then tens. Then the ones in the glass case
I stared at, who
stared back. Cotton batting

in there, and dust. I keep rubbing my ears at night,
like the baby books all say
is a sign of an infant's
infection. *Because, poor things, they
can't tell you.* But past
the faint, witless buzzing I make out
dark's quiet, open window,
rustling of leaves. Another turn
is coming up. I can hear the roar of years
falling, a crushing, hopeless momentum about to slip
into whatever's next. I had
a dream one night. The passenger pigeon's
loves were vast and particular—the great beech
forests of the middle west; countless
stands of white oak and black oak, chestnut, river birch

and elm—nearly all
of it gone. The scent of cumin
called them down, roses, coriander, caraway, anise.
And the salty snails, the perfect barely visible
workaday ant. A litany of things sweet
and small—huckleberry and gooseberry, crowberry, elderberry,
the cranberry, the currant, myrtle with its
tiny bloom. This
I didn't dream but drifted toward, the way
a room dims in twilight and the eyes
give up and turn
backward toward the brain. Most
marked bird, shimmer of feather, red there,
pale blue. I tried

its original names, half-whispering *o-mi-mi*, the way
the Algonquian did. Then *me-me*, for all
the lost Chippewa. *O-me-me-oo*, for the Potawatomi.
Omimiw, for the Cree. *Jah'oow'san'on*,
for the Seneca, who sang the bird in dance,
in gesture. *Ka-ko-ee*, said the Blackfoot.
Ori'te, the Mohawk. *Pachi*, the Choctaw.
Poweatha, the Shawnee
repeated through dry woods or dank. It was
a kind of dove I saw
as my ears throbbed on distantly,
thin, colliding music. Not the dove who mourns
every dawn in the grass, whose black spot
accuses us. But the cousin who
stayed behind, and in the old engravings still
darkens whole slow pages
with its flight.

LIBRARY STEREOPTICON

Two of everything made one, like
it was easy, like bad light
made the afternoon linger. I held it
to my whole head, a mask,
or some weird device
for breathing until I saw
odd things: a bear rising up
beside a sleeping baby; a shiny street
with palm trees, rich and busy
before perspective got it
in the end.

Overhead, the fans turned slowly as swimmers
who didn't care how far
shore was or how deep the murky water. I held
the endless, the stopped,
and loved every sepia thing: books
that no one read, hundreds on their shelves
year after year of summer.
Three blocks away, my grandmother could spend
a whole day making bread, and then
that shoebox full of pictures. Bears
fierce like that
while every fragile thing kept sleeping.

On stormy days, I'd breathe in the petrol plant
miles out on the biggest road, the wind
strange and metal. Bread

and chemicals, books I'd never read, picture
after picture stilled
by 1928. I thought there was
a shining thread
between such things. I thought
I held the needle.

II

FASTING

Some wounds are made of feathers.
Ask the smallest woodpecker whose neck
cries out a single drop. I was startled
but it was ordinary
tapping, not ice going dark into water
as I first thought. Tiny wounds
in a tangle of branches—the berries
hurt because the snow's too white.
Or wounds blacken the whole sky; one gets
caught, gets soaked in it. I've been peaceful,
walking that way before anything started
though a voice said, the world
is flat, don't sail to the edge. Maybe
I would have believed that, would have
stood at the harbor stricken as the horizon
swallowed one ship
or two ships. Turning, I saw
blood on the wing of a blackbird,
a brief thing in flight, a marking.

TULIP TREE

Some things aren't meant.
Some things aren't plain.
I planted it thinking, just

in case, the giant elms
on either side are riddled old
and ticking, sentinels

thick with shade. It seemed
tiny then. Cars crept by, all
dwarfed it deeper. One brief wind

would rattle it. Some things
aren't meant but we
were careful. The hose lay

cool and coiled and seeped
those nights until the sidewalk
rivered up, or laked.

We thought: in case, in case,
but either side so thick with shade.
Some things aren't meant—its leaf,

half almost square, half some other
shiny figure, lovely to the touch,
exactly as a letter turns, page

by page, read outside
on broken steps. I planted in that spot,
laid the hose so close, good snake

humbled by its ancient fall
from grace. It seeped past night.
Cars crept by but kids

walking liked to take a branch
or twig, thinking to play
at knives, or thinking vastly

not anything at all. It was small.
It lorded over nothing
and gave no shade. But each leaf

kept its distant kingdom
of vein and gloss. Insects never
armied it. And the snake hissed its love

all night sometimes. I forgot
and then remembered it.
We passed it daily coming

from the car. Some things
aren't meant. And even dying elms have
their duty, their everlasting shade

coming down like rain to block
the sun. I chose the spot. I watched
it leaf. One reads outside

on broken steps words dark
and light that drift
into the body and disappear.

It slowly turned away
like that. Kids walking by would
reach and break. It lorded

over nothing. Some things aren't
meant, or seem plain enough.
But I forget, then remember it.

LAMENT

At Safeway, on ice, the octopus—
great bulbous purple head
folded over, arms too many
and haphazard, pulled up like someone needed
to sweep the gleaming case *right now*.
Among tidy shrimp
and yawning tuna, it's the sideshow
freak, a thing
stopped and falling through
everything it was, past
strange to terrible to odd, dim star
between sun and moon though
the sky's all wrong, neither
day or night,
this cool fluorescence.

How old is he? I ask the kid
behind the counter, who shrugs, who
half-smiles. I look for the eye buried
in the blue-green folds. So many
eons in there. So many years
like shifting color turned to charm
the eternal underwater where it might
be asleep like that, or simply pretending—
Awful eerie sea life morgue....

But what if I claimed
the body? What if I took it and kept

walking, crossing the dismal
parking lot, its weight against me, dear
tangle of arms in its
paper shroud. What if I stood then
and fumbled with the keys, and gave it
to the darkness
filling the old back seat.
And blessed it twice, the second time
too long and endless
as water. What then—
And who would I be. And where
would I drive.

I PAINT MY BAD PAINTING

Hawaii, 1993-94

The usual accident—
blue wash on red goes purple while
swimmers move beyond me
in the water, down there against the bay's
white rush. They pray
for something threatening.
I know they do. But probably not
the plane, flying sideways just beyond
their looking up.
They miss a wave like that,
looking up.
                    Afternoon. It's getting
hotter though the ironwoods above me
release their shade. It's
branch by branch. Still, howbeit slowly,
the sun takes hold
of half the body—one arm, one leg—
and does its bleaching thing, unambiguous,
bloodless.
                    Say perhaps: I have
hopes, not many. A few, as in *a few good
nights of sleep*, or *a few
stray thoughts*, rag or paper or all the way
to bone. Now and then a no,
a yes. This painting doesn't have
enough *no* in it, I can hear
the phantom teacher saying
as she gazes past it, out that window
years ago where someone expertly stole

some poor kid's bike: quick angle
of the cutter, steely tic
of *mine all mine*.
                        It is
lovely here. One could fill a letter with it,
easy—the blue intricate,
endless, and one can't take
one's eyes from where the islands turn, risen
in the sea, a thing
gradually remembered. As I
watched from another distance once, affection
slow and muffled in me, a sound
the real heart makes. It wasn't a day
like this but fall, and I loved
both women walking and talking and leaning
toward each other on a lower street. One of them
is gone. I can't begin
to know what took
her back. The *no* in every beauty
is half delirious, half
a blinding door. She forgot us for a moment
and walked straight toward it. Sometimes
I stare and stare at things, except

                        •••

these mornings in the dark. It's not
grief exactly, lying in the big bed
this corner made of windows, house
high above the valley, the streetlight lights
scattered below like so much
glowing change. Say, 5 a.m. and up this hill,
where the road rounds the Chinese graveyard,
the garbage truck grinds its way

by headlights jacked so dim
you know by sound alone. It stops,
the men cry out—thick, jagged—not
music, more a puncture
of all that nothing that fills the head
in this dream of waking up. They leap
and the truck roars up like a creature
struck. Then quiet in its somber
wave comes back, quiet
the dead own as we own air, taking in
and breathing out the gift,
careless with it

●●●

though once I had a better story. For weeks,
my great grandmother, Nancy Gill, sick
and frail, moved in and out
of knowing anything. It was my mother's
cousins' turn to watch all night. About 1930,
in their teens, or maybe twenty, Marjorie, then Elinor—
most loved, my favorite—got crazy, the way
something small and silly strikes sometimes,
their holding back, delicious ache, before
rushing into laughter, then holding
back again, again, until they nearly
wept with nonsense.
All the while, their grandmother
lay there—*dying*, Elinor said, nearly eighty when
she told me, *while we*
laughed ourselves sick! They heard
her shift. The girls looked closer.
And Nancy Gill, herself about a hundred,
touched Elinor's face, her own face

a sudden universe
of light: *Sally, oh you've come!,* and slipped away.
Sally was her
childhood friend. *Imagine that,* Elinor said, *I was*
Sally. Our laughter called her back.
And now, some sixty years beyond that moment, this
story is an offering I make, like
oranges we see
on the Chinese graves, my son and I
walking up from school
these afternoons.
                    How many revelations do we get
a lifetime? A declaration
half-whispered, dear funny solemn secret.
My cousin told me on a fluke perhaps,
but leaning forward to touch my face so
searchingly, to be
Nancy Gill for me, she became
herself. Now I wonder at how we all so easily
flower into something *other,* odd
and wrenching slippage
world to world, laughter to that
urgent recognition. Every day we look
for oranges when we round
that wooded corner and come upon
the graves. Recompense, or mourning.
For an instant, they're
too bright for that. They sting
the eye blind

                    •••

and private. Like the sound of *A* the whole youth
orchestra tuning up

takes into wood, a hum
that goes like water, too many years
to count. I watch these
children at violin, at cello, children who
already know a simple darkness
in their hands, a thing that draws the bow
one realm to another, quick notes into
held notes like the swift descent of fever,
its hanging on until one
gives in, and hovers there.
And the young lithe director, herself
half air, half muscle, cuts the dream
with one hand up
                              for closure.
But still that world continues
somewhere in the body, in its
moonless night. How many times have I turned death
backwards in just this place? And heard
this sound? And wanted nothing
but the slow-motion
each memory makes against that *no* and *no* and *no*.
That a certain laughter does it—how? Or the fine
drift of cigarette, or the way
a stranger walks in any hallway to take us
rooms or years away. Same heart, it hangs
suspended as the children go their tangled
note by note that my son will later say
he forgot about and drifted off, waking
abruptly at the end, not knowing
what he played or who

                    •••

he was. My box of paints gets smaller. I have one
pocket-sized, and sometimes on the porch

of an afternoon, I arrange the paper and try
to paint exactly what I see—the bananas' shadow
in the broken leaves, the huge high
blooming trees beyond, and further
where the Chinese graves begin. Failing that,
there's the pure instant
when brush hits, and the paper
drinks and drinks until the blue-green
rests there. What I mean is,
so many things unsaid.

THE DOVE

Not that it's easy to keep certain moments,
not that anything in the underworld
is evident except in shards, in bits
of feathers. How the barred dove came
to Hawaii—the striped one, the zebra one—
I never found out though its markings
are an ancient dappling, a way
to disappear in so much light and so much
shade. My son came home from school
walking. I could see him from the usual
distance, up the hill and past
the graveyard. I waited for his stories
because he liked to tell me things. How he walked,
bent forward under his bookbag, stopping
to examine a stone or a crumpled note—impossible
to tell anything in his day different, that
the fourth grade boys had stalked the dove
to the lavatory slowly so it wouldn't panic.
Of course, it panicked—what wouldn't?—
which made them laugh. A few of them
had sticks, and one a brick. Recess, and my son
just stopped there after kickball. The flash
of the thing, figured out in a second but
too many of them, he said to me, Mama,
I couldn't, too many. The rest of the day,
in class, at lunch, it was upturned wings,
the bloody zig-zag hard against rafters,
down again, the sound of boys

in their glee, keeping it all back, keeping it,
until bursting into the door, into my arms—not
anything he'd done for a while, being older,
the world mostly amusing
or amazing—
And it flew then, a circling
tight in both of us. Soundless. A descent.

LATE WINTER FOG

One might be drunk
to walk down to the street. The world is
half cloud. Trees fill,
held up by it.
This creature that moves without bones.
This thing that only seems
like light.

The sound of a car, then the car,
then not. Their lowbeams—
the way eyes watch in woods from thick brush,
middle branches. A languid suspense
to walk through it.
If the world is smoke
then I must be.

A few girls
laugh and shout down the street, the constant
spring hit of the ball
they bounce. They're under
this water, as useless,
as perfect. What girls
we were, not thinking about it,
not thinking.
The mind's murky sugar
goes for blocks and blocks.

At the corner they turn. A streak
of sleeve—blue, I think.
It's the ball rising
and falling that weeps.

FISH

Under the sewage bridge, where everything
turned echo and cool, two men stared
into the filth for fish, though not
an inch of that stream
was blue, not a handful of stone
the right original color, and all
things scattered
like stars—old cans and wire,
and rusted TV tables—no,
never glistened.
But those men had nets and lines,
all the usual stuff: a beat-up
truck braked high
under the long-leafed
whatever tree that was. To be slow
then alert to the frantic ones, big
enough for the shallow part—
they wanted things
with eyes.

So they stalked
and quick, it was smothered
to the silver pail. Hardly a word
between them because anything under a bridge
is endless. A hook,
a net: there are ways
to be haunted worse.
But those fish

that ate whatever clotted thing
lay for weeks in water—

all this time, and still
mornings, or afternoons, light pooling
certain ways. That awful pulse
against the metal bucket. Sometimes
at night. In my sleep even.

AUBADE

Rain. And the birds—one
sings as an acrobat might
fake a fall
downstairs—every seasick turn
graceful unto
the farthest landing. But rain
carries its weight
straight down, as sadness does,
falling through a thought
to flood a room.

Listen to the yard. One song
builds and one unravels. Because I
dare not move, because you're
sleeping now as you never do.
I know that lantern light
in you, and dawn is bird
by bird. Rain
loves it dark and makes
a sea.

III

HEAD OF AN UNKNOWN SAINT

"Most likely used as a home shrine"
—Academy of Arts, Honolulu

He looks addled, or maybe
the paint has simply worn off the iris
of each eye until everything's
gone inward. Poor thing, life-sized
and left here like a puppet. He's wood.
He's full of curious lines where
someone cut then smoothed, then
cut again, some uncle who was best
quiet at things that could be
praised simply. I'd praise that way.
I'd say: if he looks tired, it's the weight
of goodness, not centuries. If he looks
dear somehow, it's because he loved
everything, regardless of its worth
or its chance for eternity. And the rain
at the window—never mind that it rotted
the left side of him or that insects
made a kingdom of his ear. He heard
their buzzing but it was pleasant, the tree
he'd been, the way he kept
mistaking them for wind nuzzling leaf
into leaf, so long ago, before
all this afterlife....

HOSPITAL GREENHOUSE

Here is where the old come,
suddenly fortunate
among flowers, to putter about
and forget that one good eye means
one bad one, their wish to be
doing something held low
like a leash.

But to walk here is to have
the breath sucked out. It's all
medicine, a directive
on a chart. Breathe. Breathe
as a drum might, coming up quickly
from the genius
blow of the stick. Late afternoon
the place is empty, everything
viney and stale.

Next door in real rooms, those
diligent few who dug up roots
and stared too hard
are hard at dreaming now, dozing
in bed or in a chair
until supper. Maybe it's
nothing—you close
the good eye and they both
give way. The smallest
garden. Whatever angel at the gate.

SMOKING

I don't regret it, not smoking,
though times in my twenties, I couldn't sit
through a movie whole. Halfway,
at the crucial second that weird sucked-up
feeling would come over me, and I'd bolt
to the lobby, find one of those ancient
nubby couches, smoke
going clear for the interior, down every
unlit passage until I was
normal again, fit for all those strangers
on the screen. But still out there, still sunk
to that pleasure, I'd drift into the great
boredom of the popcorn boy and the ticket girl,
that languid ache
of a place when everyone's
elsewhere—if only the next room—
stalled, distracted into themselves. I'd sit
and smoke quietly, and they'd talk
to each other, flirt even. The popcorn boy
always had a trick he'd do, stacking
Dots or Milk Duds until one box, quick,
would vanish. And the ticket girl would
lean into his counter, just so,
amused, disbelieving. *Sure*, she'd say,
and I'm Yoko Ono. Those little dramas of pure smoke,
I miss them—two real voices in those old
wedding cake theaters of the 20s, Chicago, 1973,
before they were razed for a thing

gleaming, steel and glass, when everyone
in the next room kept looking
one way, and by the bad light above me, I was
looking in, or looking down, or looking toward
these two, the dearest nothing
suspended between them.

THE EXTERMINATOR

The exterminator comes with his
circus tent and wraps up the house, whistling something
odd but not
Bach, this the simplest of Tuesdays
neither sunny nor
athrob with gloom.
Little doomed creatures somewhere near only
follow the smell of something. A crumb something.
A piece of whatever-broke-off-and-fell-
behind something. They go in steady
ancient lines for it, pitched forward
under lathe and board. Tiniest
first things!—in the wall, beneath the stairs,
living out their all-in-a-line.
We walk by and see only
stripes on the tent, and a man
in a glorious jumpsuit. A kid in a t-shirt
leans back on a car, chewing gum,
the eternal assistant, bored
as anyone with a future. And the jumpsuit guy—
he may love the fumes, who knows?—is
setting down the lines of poison, just so,
from the massive pump on wheels
in the driveway. The pump—
the pump is neither brain
nor heart. But how
careful he is, checking
panels and knobs, speaking quietly

to the machine and then to the boy and then
to himself. Imagine
the darkened house, the vast
unknowing there, little
by little.

At The Watercolor Gallery

It's not color I want but the white
of the paper left where the sky
is quietest, beyond the small tint that makes clouds,
beyond all that
exhausting attention. So a handkerchief
barely suggested in a pocket—its white
is forgetfulness. Or snow drifting against the backsteps—
one's given up.
                    On tables, at cupboards,
white is every cherished distance
in the apple, in bread, now cut
and abandoned, as if someone
heard a voice
and went to it. And always the knife—
the part that shines
is empty.
                    Outside again, it's
in the pale underbelly of a bird, or brief
on its wing extended like that
over fields, over reef and water—memory, sure,
though we were
never there, in that kitchen or on that
brutal coastal rock.
                        It's all a lie, except
these bits and drifts of nothing, where
brush never bothered, nor color
insisted—the calm white
in the eye of the girl in the portrait
where the world has no hope, no
work to do.

Waiting Out The Music Lesson

Somewhere down the hall, he is playing cello
against his teacher's furious piano.
But across from me a woman dozes—
as usual, head back,
mouth open—this vaguest hour
of the afternoon. Her daughter is behind the door
marked *Willow*. A violin in there,
two violins, the teacher stopping them
and starting them as 1-2-3 as anyone out to find
what shorts the damaged circuit.
Children wait their turn
on benches, or across the way—viola
in a canvas bag, box
of flute. All of us
stare down the doves that land
in this open hallway, one boy with his
rubber band pulled back, ready.

This could be a flash
of the afterlife, or the famous
deathbed second, all mystery
reduced to one simple
ordinary cube. Afternoons with neither
genius or grandeur. . . . The boy's aim is bad, the bird
startled though not convinced.
But the dreamer, her eyes closed
every week I've come, is as pale as some
thought I can't get by, something
that refuses to be clear.

FIREWORKS AT NEW YEAR

So the flame tells the night briefly
not a secret but the one
private thing it knows. Above houses
darkness is, then isn't....
Fire, down for months
in its paper shroud until a hand
finds a match, the turning year: a compliance,
fierce.
      It's over. Of course
instantly. But the eye keeps on
seeing it there, the high
bright spill. Seeing it there,
and seeing it, what it was like,
that desire.

The American Opera Company

Forty years running, it boiled down by then
to one backdrop, a garden
faded to an afterlife of flowers
rolled up in Madame's little studio. Below
the lesser end of Chicago's elegant
Michigan Avenue, such muted glitter, and beyond
the ancient lake. My brother, just
a kid, 14, came every Saturday
to be *Aida*'s king or *Boheme*'s Rodolfo.
And the tiny Madame Del Prado,
squeezed in behind her giant grand, played
each riff—again, Michael!—a hundred times.
Then those sandwiches she'd make, something
out of a tin, deviled ham
or corned beef, so salty
they dazed on the thick brown bread.
And of course, this triumph
or that—Venice, Frankfort,
three cities in New Jersey, 1933—such
hopeless radiance on stage, even the men
would weep.

Is it the gasoline air that makes
this stay? We all went home in that.
But my brother alone, the el and two buses,
his whole head maybe, a pure B sharp.
Over and over her note at the piano—here Michael,
here—and he'd hit it

and keep it. How strangers burned away.
My brother telling me
years later, the train's odd sad pitch—E flat—
and braking at the grimy stations, a low D
so sudden and eerie. Real, it happened,
but now this much a story: one boy, mid-century,
silent except for singing
in that room of ghosts. The old woman
rapt with—what?—not herself,
not even music. I saw that backdrop once,
how the path lost itself in flowers—nothing to do
with the plot, or with the bursting,
chanting mob downstage,
oblivious, on and on.

Old Ball Field

Birds suddenly forlorn in such a field, school hours,
so the land empties itself
back to simple pasture. A flock of sparrows, and then
another flock descend and rise, descend
and rise haphazard. This one,
that one there.

It's probably the light. Late morning,
cloudy, and the birds too hungry because
it's spring. *It's spring,* says
the silent couple in the dugout, three hours now
of skipping school, and kissing there,
not an eye between them open.

THE BAY WATERS

A thousand times I wanted to be
elsewhere. There are windows for that,
and rain. Or even today, spring
narrowing down to a simple desire, those two
with their kids and a dog
on the wharf, and now an old man who can't decide
to sit or stand. A boat to rent.
They've been at it for hours, but really
I could have told them. Everyone wanting
to go out in it, something like
tinfoil gone languid, something that only seems
the hard truth—shattering, pulling back. So the long-lost
dogged grace blood must have
over the same route year after year, a lifetime
to bring down the frail tubing
and wash. This wish to go inward. We talk
about water, talk to it. It's breathing
like we are. It's cold
then warm.
                  Like yesterday, I found
the abandoned restaurant at the harbor, broken windows,
but booths still upright, full
of sea air like spit. Boats docked there, rocking
and rocking as if singing
or dreaming. Thursday, the light milky,
late afternoon. I walked there like the last
left thing on earth because it *is* spring
and one defies in spring

the way flowers never forgive the earth for their
kept life underground. They do anything, any color,
to fly out of it. So the restaurant—
over and done with—but I could see it
like some pale thing in the dark though it wasn't dark,
old customers in a better season, softening
over beer and whiskey, waiting for boats.
Just the slightest shrug, the body
tuned to an alert so quiet, between two lives,
the ordinary one and the hidden one—a glimpse
on such an afternoon,
a ruined place like that....
                         Most of the morning, I've
watched the small cars
between trees and white buildings
all down the bay. An island, a second island, then three
and four and five out to sea, bridge to silver
bridge like music doubts and doubles back, trees
big enough to count. And still
the bay waters, all multitude, drugged
blue-green glass.
                    The dog's knotted
black as sea rope. He lunges toward land, whistled
back because—who knows?—it might be
any minute now. Everyone looks up—so many clouds—
and the old man perhaps wonders if it's too
windy to go out, if it's really
too windy.
I hear this: fog horns
and gulls, little razors at an angle. I pretend
to hear other things: a runner as she
takes the bridge, or distant valves and brakes,
or the small circle of talk,

then nothing, a word or two, then
nothing—those few
with their dog and their patience, their coolers
and rods and their slow tin buckets.
                                        But one loves most
what one loves
without thinking. Clouds thickening the bay
seal it steadily in shadow and drown
the bright quicksilver, the whole going out, the coming back.
Such dark must be
what the deaf hear, everything disguised by faint buzzes
and grindings and clicks—water
below this water, and fish we can't see
swimming in strange obsessive patterns because
they never know light.
And deep enough, earth, its red furious wish
to be another element that flows
and burns, and is
terrible, and is secret.
                        I mean, they simply
wait for a boat.
One kid throws a stick in the water. The other
stands there, pointing.

BY THE SEA

Waterglasses shine in the small cafe.
For breakfast, only one or two
in there this early. A woman holds her spoon
just so and it catches
light like the needle taking thread.
Morning sun. Of course
it falls in stripes, at angles
though whole sections of the sandy walk
pool with it.
                But it's all shadow by the rocks
or just a slower water where a man
stands to throw his line
too far, into the whirling
spitting surf. What fish would dare?
He has that
secret sullen look of anyone
up since four
to plumb all this.
                The flimsy plastic chairs
everywhere down the beach are empty, a few
blown over, wind or something.
I love how
white they are, so many facing outward as if
absently in wait
for what is glorious.
                Or something drastic
in the sea. Already a boy's out there, a flash
of him barely visible on his board.

Two Umbrellas

—as if someone, stunned, had
hurried off and left them,
breadcrumbs, clues,
where the yard angled down past the bottom terrace
and banana trees began. The open one,
all blue geometry, a woodcut
off the block. The other, loose
and closed, the darkest pink.
                              Two days
and then they vanished—another mystery.
Two days to make
the backyard strange. Looking down, I remembered
now and then to love
them there, perfect excess,
perfect ease and zero explanation.
                              We tried: *umbrellas*

blown off someone's porch. But whose?
Only trees there, and then
the leaves gave way to nothing
we could see.
                 Instead, this dream
came twice to me, once awake and once asleep: two
lost girls cutting through the vast dark
undergrowth below, and coming out—maybe
it seemed like days
and days in there—to find
anything too much
to carry.

Or it's easy—
sweet sudden throwing down
of something.

EXHAUSTION

Snow lay like exhaustion
all over the yard. Then why
this thrill waking up to see it
as though some
large mystery had given up
and said *here*.
Snow, the slow boat. The great
tiredness in it
is a haven the way
great loss is a haven.
No one does it deliberately
but one gets brought to this
as though to an altar
at the beginning of winter.
Where I walked all fall aspen leaves,
poplar, maple
stained the sidewalk. Their fate
is to become
something else. One foot and one foot
and one foot. The way
is deeper now and the leaves
are under all of it.
I would like to say
I could hear them, that the leaves
love to sing and have
many songs under the snow.
I would like to say
all kinds of nonsense.

X-Ray Vision

is what my brother longed for, clipping out
his coupon from the screwy comic,
longed for and paid for, one solid
quarter beneath the cellophane tape.
Then he waited day and night
for sight. *Right through clothes*: oh monstrous,
miniature scope in the hand to set the eye
to all things in the world
delicious and forbidden, under something
vastly, boringly
not. *Allow six weeks*, he
kept intoning. Hope, not litany
though certainly it was prayer. (I can
see, cried the trembling
blind man in the movie for our Catholic
fifth grade, our teacher half
weeping as the projector
spit and smoked and nearly burned up....)

At home it was simply
any mail? Week after week my brother
sailing through the door. Our poor mother
with her *no* aimed at his back,
exact. I said, could you see
through cats' fur? Through a door
of steel? Something quick like an eyelid,
quicker, like a bird,
like the wing, down to its bones

and glue? *Anything, moron*—he
forever patient, still
patient. O invincible
country, where childhood is,
and faith, a little
masterpiece.

A SMALL THING

Everyone is squinting
at the beach. Sand gives way to ironwoods—
trees like pine but they are not.
And water—the legendary blue is halfway
green, like bronze
forgotten in a drawer. Enormous yachts
so far away seem
small, the way they thinly look the part
of exquisite taste.

Which is to say, here on the local beach,
you bring a lunch or you don't eat.
There's a changing room. An outdoor shower
with two leaky spitting faucets.
That's it. For some, too much
who keep their salt
and go home afternoons, the ocean
still on their skin and tangled
soggy in their hair.

One girl's been here for hours. She's left
a castle now, two moats, the surf
spinning in and out. Its towers
gloat above all turbulence,
like years and years turn slowly
into history. I saw her
father bored, looking out

to the blue expanse before
they turned to find their car in a sea
of cars. The twig?
The twig's a flag.

HOME VIDEOS OF THE HURRICANE

—Kokee State Park Natural
Museum, Kauai

It starts out funny: his own house
shattered, he turns to the neighbor's—*Holy Jesus,*
there goes Frank's roof. A trillion
billion particles an hour: bits of shingle, shards
of lathe and wallboard, the fabulous
souvenir lampshade soaring off.
Soon enough the steeple of whatever church
explodes, the spirit life
gone TNT. Just wait.
Trees uproot. Bushes fly drugged
as anything with wings
after a glut of certain berries.
And gradually, and quick as light,
fear fills up
the small museum, people standing or sitting still
to watch the ruin
even as we speak. No one speaks.
We gape and breathe
too hard—nothing
Hollywood could manage, this bit by bit,
everyone's ragged version
pieced together, a hellish quilt. That
fascinates, that
rules the mob of us
down to a quiet sugar. It's the windows

I'll remember, their long X's
made of tape, just
before. A kind of prayer—*o spare us*—not
what it really was, target
after target.

ABOVE THE CHINESE CEMETERY

Rain, and fireworks every morning this week,
a flaming bucket
on one of the graves they keep
throwing things into. So the family in white t-shirts
bend and bow
behind the young tree rioting
pink blossoms. Hard to know
exactly—except for their blue and white
umbrellas. Except
the fire.
          But slowly, smoke and incense
climb the hill to our house. I pick out of the wind
their prayer chant.
                    April, month
of flowers and candy and fruit
for the dead. I've found cake down there
on the stones at nightfall, its icing
an astonishing blue. And Hershey kisses in shiny foil.
And plain bread. And plain oranges.
In rain, the younger ones
are sent to the car
to wait.
          But their parents, still grieving,
work the round of small explosives
to keep the soul heavenward. It snaps and burns and bursts
like a bad gun, like some wayward
stricken drunk shooting straight up. *Dear father,*
mother. What sound in the world

isn't weeping? Even as rain
comes harder or faster, and wind
makes a flickering heart
of the fire....

IN YOUR GARDEN

The plane passed over and I lost
track of what you said.
I had a childhood like that
at the edge of the city.
But you kept talking even as I
pointed at the sky, cupping my ear
toward you, just so.
                    Third anniversary
of your death. So I remember as a kid, world
frozen by this same numbing
airborne roar. Though not
everything, as if
a ball could ever stop mid-air its bounce,
small quarrels their rage, or anyone
a day of summer....
               But your words
came back. You were showing me
all that loves the shade—the hosta,
the columbine,
of course the bleeding heart, each
so perfectly wrought, as though
born of some machine
that makes tragedy ordinary
and eternal, and hanging
by a thread.
           I only know you
touched my arm—what?—and finally turned
to see the plane diminished.
Oh, hardly a threat, you said.

After Surgery

I couldn't read. Mostly I'd drift, half awake
because drugs hung limp from the pole,
their little crackling sacks. I'd look up to a nurse
stationed at the door, counting my breathing,
my rising and falling, writing it down. On good days,
I'd catch her and hold
my air back, or speed it up, and *you!* she'd say
and we'd both laugh though it
hurt to laugh. Always, the shunt at my hip,
its slow welling up of blood, little vinyl
handgrenade they'd drain to measure, then
shake their heads and put it back
empty but the leak out of me would
keep up, keep up. I had favorites
among the nurses—one walked me
down the hall each day, a very big deal,
like Columbus sighting land, or Henry Hudson
not abandoned after all at his famous
hopeless waters. Not exactly
happy endings but just to get through
a day of that, and another day, and so on.
Well, there's no embarrassment
like the bathroom with a nurse
standing there, when the body half-works
and drugs rear up in the belly, and whatever
else locks in reverse, or inside out,
or never to be. She was cheerfully
unimpressed by such misery, matter-of-fact because

routine is a kindness, or maybe hope, maybe
its highest manifestation. Manifest: to
make clear, to show itself, from the Latin
manifestus, "hit by the hand." There were times
I stood blank, bloated, down
the long suck of everlasting worthlessness
or where the self just stopped at some vast
nothing—two different things but one gives
into the other, like an uncle and an aunt,
one low-pitched, one high-pitched, one
who kept talking, one who never
spoke to children. I wasn't
myself, as they say. Or I was myself utterly,
for the first time. One dissolves
like a bad pill. One can't bear it
another minute.
                    The night nurse rolled
through such darkness the way certain large women
hover, unexpectedly graceful. She had
a flashlight, checking each hour how
the I.V. was dripping, or if the morphine
was doing the job—not morphine, which made me
sicker, something else—or my shunt, filling up
the handgrenade, whether it was
getting pinker, a good sign. She glided in
on the pale line cast
by the hall, door crooked
a little, but her flashlight—I was
one dim thought, that's all, distant
in that dark as earth
from any other planet. And she was orbiting endlessly,
or she was a comet approaching.

FLOWERS

How flowers exaggerate. Neither
rain gives cause, nor
light all day and all day—
a blue with such misfortune in it,
red with its
deliberate ecstasy. And the yellow
which goes inward
to forget *why flowers at all.*
Why anything.
So I stood once in a garden
thinking as far as a thought could go,
to childhood and back. And then
ahead where the old woman
watered patiently. I watched how
careful she was, and silent,
disappearing between the bellflower
and the late lilies, the water
nothing that opened but it
brought things: the shine
of a leaf, the earth
pooling, then giving in
to take and take. A muffled
constant sound. The sound
of sorrow speeded up
or slowed down so utterly
I could hear the monotony
of love in it. Same
same water, sweet,
dangerous. The flowers lie back
in the weight of it.

CELLO

So the rusted jamb
works anyway, the door left open.
And the floor, complaining,
nevertheless takes each
human step. Narrow stairs
in the house seem
a ladder, too steep, and day
by day, not as angels climb
each step, each step.
So a child takes up the cello
and puts it down and takes it up,
there, upstairs, its deep ways
drawn gradually where
breath is slow
or not at all. Sound
of wood thinned and pressed
to the shape he holds: how many
afternoons there, an hour
in the long half shade.
Rosin the bow, she said.
Alone now, he stops
and rubs the horsehair with the care
of a child remembering, serious for once,
not distracted, taking his time
because he loves his teacher
which is to say, he
believes her. The tree gave up its

wood and sap, not willingly
but everything softens in his hand—
the long reach, the bow's
resistance.

Old Cemetery

Before she said no, dear girl, I can't forever,
I came with her straight to this tree
where most of ours are buried, clouds
dragging their business slower,
bigger on the grass, one bird throwing down
its shadow flying, whirled confetti
in its beak. Then a thing
would click to make
another thing: this time and
that time, who said it, who didn't.
Exactly what—I don't know
what I know. There was silence.
Or it was just my grandmother shaking her head.
So the quiet ones could talk,
she reached back. Say
it is possible. Say they were busy
in the next world, and we were here,
it was summer, late afternoon
the thinnest veil to lift.

YEAR IN HAWAII

The ocean takes so long
to think about. I was a toad
there, a river thing that got
lost somewhere between one rearing up
and the next, the surf
before it blinded altogether. Distance
stops; one sees the endless line
of something though mostly a boat out there
is simple, with an oar or with a sail.
I never had a vision
about the place. I never thought: this
is the beginning of the world. I watched
birds. I watched the graceless
albatross. And the sea repeated itself
the way blood brings
its bounty to the heart
and the heart knocks back. So much
of beauty is the same. You've seen
the postcards. People buy them thinking
everything worthwhile comes
through a camera lens, and they put them
in a pocket or down the dark throat
of a mailbox someone later opens
with a key. I've watched tourists
some. I've watched how they love it all,
how tired they get loving it, wishing
they were a little farther
down the beach. And the Hawaiians

wanting just to live there, thank you,
going off to work and coming back, normal
things. I was 43 which doesn't mean
much except I wasn't young
and I wasn't old staring into the sea
which changed exactly because it
did not change. There's a way such
beauty refuses to be anything
other than itself, some god
one might have worshipped in another life.
The scent of that worship's
everywhere. The flowers breathe
it back, and the trees are far too
tangled than they need to be, like people
who dream too much, and hour after hour
never stop turning in their beds. I wanted to
sit on a rock and write down something.
I wanted to have a thought
that would throw itself to danger,
a blazing sacrifice. But beauty
doesn't take you places. I liked the rock
I chose. I could see the others better.
They made a little hook out there, and farther down
a coastline. Months of that. And people say,
it was paradise, wasn't it?
And I think of Eden before the original
wrong turn. I remember it now, I do,
though it's not longing that comes over me
but Eve's restlessness again, the way coral lives
near shore, dark and whorled
as a human brain, at risk
and breaking.

NEST

I walked out, and the nest
was already there by the step. Woven basket
of a saint
sent back to life as a bird
who proceeded to make
a mess of things. Wind
right through it, and any eggs
long vanished. But in my hand it was
intricate pleasure, even the thorny reeds
softened in the weave. And the fading
leaf mold, hardly
itself anymore, merely a trick
of light, if light
can be tricked. Deep in a life
is another life. I walked out, the nest
already by the step.

ACKNOWLEDGMENTS

The New England Review Crushed Birds
           At the Watercolor Gallery
           By the Sea
           Sewing
           In the Street, Men Working

Field   Lament
           Hospital Greenhouse
           I Notice on My Walk
           Momentary, in Winter
           Halfway
           After Surgery
           Head of an Unknown Saint
           Fasting
           Home Videos of the Hurricane
           Nest
           The Exterminator
           Fish

The American Voice   Stained Glass Windows
           Nesting Boxes
           Flowers
           Cello
           Snow Falling

Massachusetts Review   Car Covered with Snow
           Library Stereopticon

Iowa Review	The American Opera Company
	Old Ball Field
	Aubade
	Exhaustion
	Bird Passing
Georgia Review	The Vietnam Birthday Lottery, 1970
	Happiness
Virginia Quarterly Review	Above the Chinese Cemetery
	A Small Thing
The Southern Review	The Great Ape House
American Poetry Review	Lent
Boulevard	Late Winter Fog
Denver Quarterly	The Book of Hand Shadows
	X-Ray Vision
	Chinese Brushwork
Northwest Review	The Bay Waters
	Waiting Out the Music Lesson
Pequod	Year in Hawaii
	The Dove
Talking River Review	In Your Garden
Verse	Swimming Lesson
	Omens

Shenandoah	Camouflage
	The Hawk
The Kenyon Review	I Paint My Bad Painting
The Salt Hill Review	Tulip Tree
	Two Umbrellas
	Fireworks at New Year

"Camouflage" appeared in *Best American Poetry, 1997.*

The author is grateful to Purdue University for the sabbatical leave, the Ragdale Foundation for the residencies, and the Center for Artistic Endeavors, School of Liberal Arts at Purdue for the fellowship, all of which aided the completion of this book. Continuing and affectionate thanks to the first readers of these poems: David Dunlap, Joy Manesiotis, and Brigit Kelly.

ABOUT THE AUTHOR

Marianne Boruch lives with her husband
and son in West Lafayette, Indiana,
where she teaches in the MFA Program in
Creative Writing at Purdue University. Her
previous books include *View from the Gazebo,
Descendant,* and *Moss Burning* (published by
Oberlin College Press in the *FIELD* Poetry
Series in 1993), and a collection of writings
on poetry, *Poetry's Old Air.*

COLOPHON

Designed by Steve Farkas.
Composed by Professional Book Compositors
using Weiss 11 point text type and 15 point
bold display type. Printed and bound by
Cushing-Malloy using 60# Glatfelter offset
acid-free paper. B-Grade black cloth on
the casebound books with silver foil
stamping on the spine.